Peel Me a Grape

Edited by Joseph Weintraub

Peel Me a Grape

Futura Publications Limited

A Futura Book

First published in Great Britain in 1975
by Futura Publications Limited

PUBLISHER'S NOTE
'Peel Me A Grape' edited by Joseph Weintraub, was
originally published under the title 'The Wit and
Wisdom of Mae West' edited by Joseph Weintraub

ISBN 0 8600 72401
Printed in Great Britain by
Hazell Watson & Viney Ltd
Aylesbury, Bucks

Futura Publications Limited
Warner Road, London SE5

ACKNOWLEDGMENTS

Stills from 'She Done Him Wrong', 'Go West, Young Man', 'Goin' to Town', and 'I'm No Angel' reproduced by arrangement with Universal City Studios Inc.

Stills from 'Tropicana' reproduced by arrangement with Columbia Pictures International Corporation.

Stills from 'Belle of the Nineties', 'Night After Night', 'Klondike Annie', 'Every Day's a Holiday' and 'My Little Chickadee' reproduced by arrangement with Paramount Pictures Corporation, and Universal Pictures.

Stills from 'Myra Breckinridge' by courtesy of Twentieth Century-Fox Film Company Limited.

Photographs 27, 28, 29 and 30 Copyright © Popperfoto
Photographs 31, 32 Copyright © Camera Press (Jerry Watson)

AUTHOR'S ACKNOWLEDGMENTS
My thanks to Dion McGregor, The Memory Shop, Carlos Clarens, Lou Valentino, Jerry Vermilye, The Museum of Modern Art, Paramount Pictures, Universal Pictures, Columbia Pictures and Prentice-Hall, Inc., publishers of *Goodness Had Nothing to Do With It* by Mae West, © 1959.

Whilst every effort has been made to trace copyright owners for photographs, we apologise if any have been omitted.

To Helen

INTRODUCTION

Mae West – the vamp of high camp – was a legend and an institution before she came to Hollywood in 1932. She helped to make the Twenties roar, brought Paramount Studios out of the red and into the blue during the depression-scarred Thirties and kept the censors raging and the crowds coming. If the censors believed that eternal vigilance was the price of decency, they didn't realize that Miss West could find a double-entendre in a lullaby. As she herself has said: 'It isn't what I do, but how I do it. It isn't what I say, but how I say it, and how I look when I do it and say it.' And so, Mae West laid the cards on the table and her curves on the couch while she purred, 'Come up and see me sometime.'

Rough, tough, vital and magnetic, Mae West is still universal in her appeal – her surface metallic, her glitter untarnished.

JOSEPH WEINTRAUB

THE BALLAD OF MAE WEST'S BUST

My eyes have seen upon life's screen
  The wreck of countless dreams,
Where'er I turn 'tis but to learn
  That naught is as it seems,
And 'neath the sun I've found but one
  Tradition I can trust:
One thing that's sure and does endure
  Is Mae West's bust . . .

My many years are wet with tears
    As down my checkered way
All I held true went up the flue
    And perished day by day;
I've viewed with grief each pet belief
    Go crumbling into dust
Till quite bereft there's nothing left
    But Mae West's bust . . .

Nor friends nor fame remain the same
    And life's a hollow shell,
I'm betting odds there are no Gods,
    Nor Paradise nor Hell;
No lucid laws, no Santa Claus;
    Injustice rules the just;
In all life's range all models change
    But Mae West's bust . . .

ANON.

MAE WEST ON STAGE

Discussing summer stock:

Summer or winter they seem to like what I do.

In one of her reviews, Miss West was told that ten men were waiting to meet her at home. She replied:

I'm tired, send one of them home.

YOU MUST BE GOOD AND TIRED?
No, just tired.

Diamond Lil is all mine and I she. She's I, and in my modest way I consider her a classic. Like *Hamlet*, sort of, but funnier.

DIAMOND LIL

People have said that I must be
bad myself because I play bad parts
so well. They fail to credit me with
intelligence and love for my art. . . .
Particularly now, when such things as
'companionate marriage' ideas
are floating around, is *Diamond Lil*
timely. I don't believe in it. I think
it is nothing more than contracted
prostitution. Marriage, love
and home should be kept sacred. . . .
I believe in the single standard
for men and women.

CATHERINE WAS GREAT

Catherine Was Great opened to hostile critics. Miss West commented:

The way the boys wrote up the show, I'm surprised they weren't raided. And to think I took out the stronger lines ... on account of Lent.

Miss West's famous curtain speech that she made after each performance of Catherine Was Great:

I'm glad you like my Catherine. I like her too. She ruled thirty million people and had three thousand lovers. I do the best I can in two hours.

CATHERINE WAS GREAT
Mae West as Catherine

When asked a question about a rebellion, Catherine answered.

What do you think I have an army for – and don't answer that.

CATHERINE: Russia needs her men – in fact I need them.

CATHERINE WAS GREAT
Mae West as Catherine

When Catherine meets Ivan VI, the man who has never seen a woman, she muses:

What a tragedy for a man, what an opportunity for a woman.

When Field Marshal Potemkin brought her news of war with the Turks, she said:

Come up to the royal suite later tonight – and we'll talk Turkey.

POTEMKIN (*while embracing Catherine*): I am yours to command.

CATHERINE: I command you to attack.

HOLLYWOOD

Miss West arrived in Hollywood in 1932 with the following remark:

I'm not a little girl from a little town making good in a big town. I'm a big girl from a big town making good in a little town.

Supporters as well as detractors of Miss West have always insisted that she was instrumental in bringing about reform and censorship. This is slightly exaggerated but she would be the first to support this theory. In reference to censorship Miss West has said:

It's hard to be funny when you have to be clean.

My advice to those girls who think they have to take
their clothes off to be a star: Baby, once you're boned,
what's to create the illusion? ... Never be obvious. Let
both the men and the women wonder. The men for
what they think they haven't got and the women for
what they know they haven't got.

HOLLYWOOD

I play the kind of dame that always asks for more than she expects to get – and then gets more than she asked for.

During the film slump of 1938 Miss West commented:

The only picture to make money recently was *Snow White and the Seven Dwarfs*, and that would have made twice as much if they had let me play Snow White.

Virtue has its own reward, but has no sale at the box office.

Why should I go good when I'm packing them in because I'm bad?

NIGHT AFTER NIGHT

Mae West as Maudie Triplett

Miss West asked to rewrite her own dialogue for her first film, Night After Night. *The following line was to be the title of her autobiography:*

HATCHECK GIRL: Goodness, what lovely diamonds.

MAUDIE TRIPLETT: Goodness had nothing to do with it, dearie.

SHE DONE HIM WRONG

Mae West as Lou

EVER MEET A MAN THAT COULD MAKE YOU HAPPY?

LOU: Several times.

No gold-digging for me . . . I take diamonds! We may be off the gold standard someday.

It takes two to get one in trouble.

I'M NO ANGEL
Mae West as Tira

I wrote the story myself. It's all about a girl who lost her reputation but never missed it.

Asked what kind of character she is playing in the film, Miss West said:

She's the kind of girl who climbed the ladder of success, wrong by wrong.

On the noted absence of stars at the opening of I'm No Angel:

Maybe they figure seeing this picture would come under the heading of homework.

When I'm No Angel *opened at Grauman's Chinese Theatre, Miss West commented:*

It's rather nice to be in a place where they take your footprints instead of your fingerprints.

I'M NO ANGEL
Mae West as Tira

In a spot where the script called for her to look bored, Miss West turned to her maid and ad libbed:

Peel me a grape, Beulah.

I'M NO ANGEL
Mae West as Tira

ASTROLOGER: I see a new position for you.

TIRA: Sitting or reclining?

I've been things and seen places.

KENT TAYLOR: When may I see you – breakfast, lunch, dinner?

TIRA: Well – I always have breakfast in bed – so that's out.

A figure with curves always offers a lot of interesting angles.

One figure can sometimes add up to a lot.

GERTRUDE MICHAEL: You haven't a streak of decency in you.

TIRA: I don't show my good points to strangers.

I'm no angel, but I've spread my wings a bit.

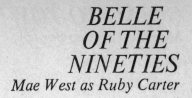

BELLE OF THE NINETIES
Mae West as Ruby Carter

A man in the house is worth two in the street.

It is better to be looked over than overlooked.

There are no good girls gone wrong; there are bad girls found out.

Keep cool and collect.

GOING TO TOWN
Mae West as Cleo Borden

CLEO: For a long time I was ashamed of the way I lived.

DID YOU REFORM?

CLEO: No, I'm not ashamed anymore.

WHERE'S THE FIRE?

CLEO: In your eyes, big boy.

I'VE BEEN DOING A LOT OF THINKING ABOUT YOU LATELY.

CLEO: You must be awful tired.

GOING TO TOWN
Mae West as Cleo Borden

YOU AIN'T SCARED OF ME BECAUSE THEY SAY I'M A BAD MAN?

CLEO: I'm a good woman for a bad man.

I'm a woman of very few words, but lots of action.

GOING TO TOWN
Mae West as Cleo Borden

I DIDN'T KNOW YOU SPEAK SPANISH?

CLEO: Don't think I worked in Tijuana for nothing.

Referring to Delilah:

I have a lot of respect for that dame. There's one lady barber that made good.

I'M THE BACKBONE OF MY FAMILY.

CLEO: Your family should see a chiropractor.

DO YOU CONSIDER YOURSELF A GOOD JUDGE OF HORSE-FLESH?

CLEO: I don't know, I never ate any.

GOING TO TOWN
Mae West as Cleo Borden

WHEN IT COMES TO YOU, I'M DYNAMITE.

CLEO: And I'm your match.

KLONDIKE ANNIE
Mae West as Frisco Doll

Between two evils, I always pick the one I never tried before.

I CAN ALWAYS TELL A LADY WHEN I SEE ONE.

FRISCO DOLL: Yeah? What do you tell 'em?

A gold rush is what happens when a line of chorus girls spot a man with a bankroll.

KLONDIKE ANNIE
Mae West as Frisco Doll

Women are as old as they feel – and men are old when they lose their feelings.

Give a man a free hand and he'll try to put it all over you.

Too many girls follow the line of least resistance – but a good line is hard to resist.

Some men are all right in their place – if they only knew the right places!

GO WEST YOUNG MAN
Mae West as Mavis Arden

A thrill a day keeps the chill away.

EVERY DAY'S
A HOLIDAY
Mae West as Peaches O'Day

Two lines famous for their double-entendre that the Hays office deleted from the film were:

I wouldn't lift my veil for that guy.

I wouldn't let him touch me with a ten-foot pole.

EVERY DAY'S
A HOLIDAY
Mae West as Peaches O'Day

I always say, keep a diary and someday it'll keep you.

It ain't no sin if you crack a few laws now and then, just so long as you don't break any.

That guy's so crooked he uses a corkscrew for a ruler.

MY LITTLE CHICKADEE

Mae West as Flower Belle Lee

Talking to an interviewer about making a Western with W.C. Fields, Miss West commented:

W. C. Fields, a great performer. My only doubts about him come in bottles.

MY LITTLE CHICKADEE

Mae West as Flower Belle Lee

I generally avoid temptation unless I can't resist it.

Every man I meet wants to protect me. I can't figure out what from.

A man's kiss is his signature.

MY LITTLE CHICKADEE

Mae West as Flower Belle Lee

I WONDER WHAT KIND OF WOMAN YOU ARE?

FLOWER BELLE: Sorry: I can't give out samples.

I was in a tight spot but managed to wriggle out of it.

JUDGE: Are you trying to show contempt for the court?

FLOWER BELLE: No, I'm doing my best to hide it.

I see you're a man with ideals. I guess I better be going while you've still got them.

MY LITTLE CHICKADEE

Mae West as Flower Belle Lee

Definition of subtraction:

A man has one hundred dollars and you leave him with two dollars, that's subtraction.

I learned early that two and two are four, and five will get you ten if you know how to work it.

CAN YOU HANDLE IT?

FLOWER BELLE: Yeah, and I can kick it around, too!

AREN'T YOU FORGETTING YOU'RE MARRIED?

FLOWER BELLE: Hmmm – I'm doing my best.

MY LITTLE CHICKADEE

Mae West as Flower Belle Lee

SPRING IS THE TIME FOR LOVE.

FLOWER BELLE: What's the matter with the rest of the year?

Any time you got nothing to do – and lots of time to do it – come on up.

MISC. WEST

Sex and I have a lot in common. I don't want to take any credit for inventing it – but I may say, in my own modest way, and in a manner of speaking, that I have rediscovered it.

I play no favorites. There's something about every man. A man may be short, dumpy, and rapidly getting bald – but if he has *fire*, women will like him.

It isn't what I do, but how I do it. It isn't what I say, but how I say it, and how I look when I do it and say it.

Many a man picks up a girl – only to fall himself.

Men admire devotion in their wives – beauty in other women.

A man in love is like a clipped coupon – it's time to cash in.

Men are all alike – except the one you've met who's different.

Whenever a guy starts boasting to me about his family tree, I seem to smell a strong sniff of sap rising.

The score never interested me, only the game.

Men are my hobby; if I ever got married I'd have to give it up.

When a man starts to alibi he usually has a pretty good reason for it – a blonde or brunette.

All discarded lovers should be given a second chance, but with somebody else.

The man I don't like doesn't exist.

Men are my kind of people. I was once asked what ten men I'd like to have come up and see me sometime. Why ten; why not a hundred, a thousand?

It's not the men in my life that counts – it's the life in my men.

It's not the man you see me with; it's the men you don't see me with.

Is that a gun in your pocket, or are you just glad to see me?

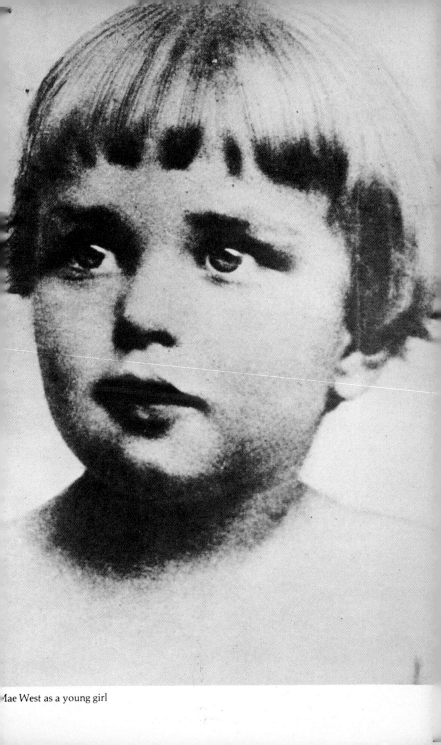

Mae West as a young girl

Mae West in a scene from 'Night After Night'
Checkroom girl: 'Goodness, what beautiful diamonds!'
Mae West: 'Goodness had nothing to do with it, dearie'

Mae West and her co-star George Raft in 'Night After Night', with Constance Cummings, Wynne Gibson and Alison Skipworth

Mae West with her leading man Cary Grant in 'She Done Him Wrong', the film which 'launched' Cary Grant

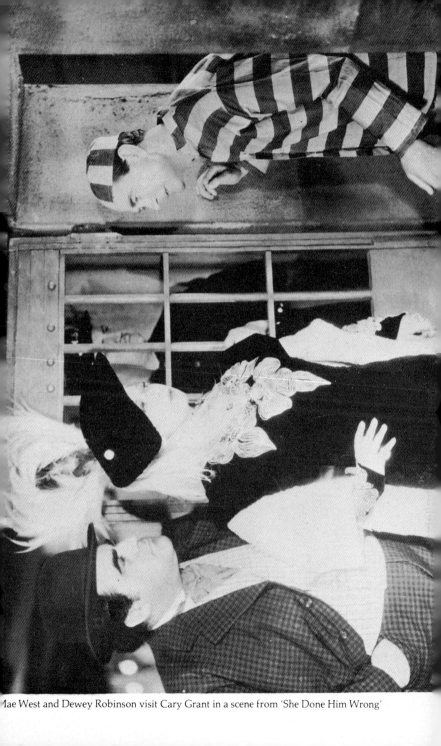

Mae West and Dewey Robinson visit Cary Grant in a scene from 'She Done Him Wrong'

Mae West demonstrates her screen love-making techniques with Cary Grant, her leading man in 'I'm No Angel'

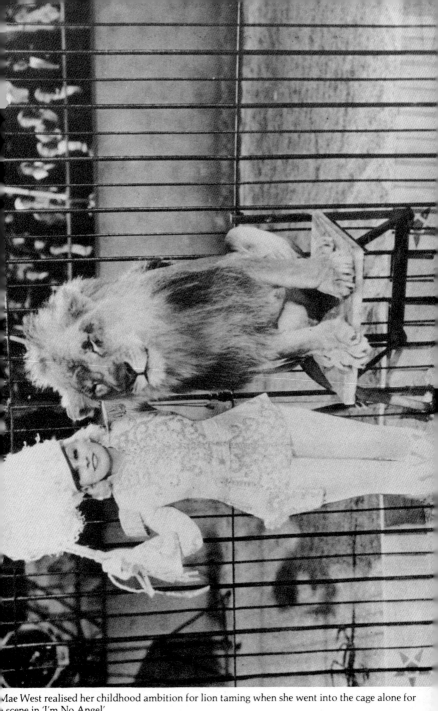

Mae West realised her childhood ambition for lion taming when she went into the cage alone for scene in 'I'm No Angel'

Mae West with John Mack Brown, one of her three leading men in 'Belle of the Nineties'

Mae West 'Goin' to Town'

Mae West had seven leading men in 'Goin' to Town' and in one scene she had to burlesque some of the opera 'Samson and Delilah'

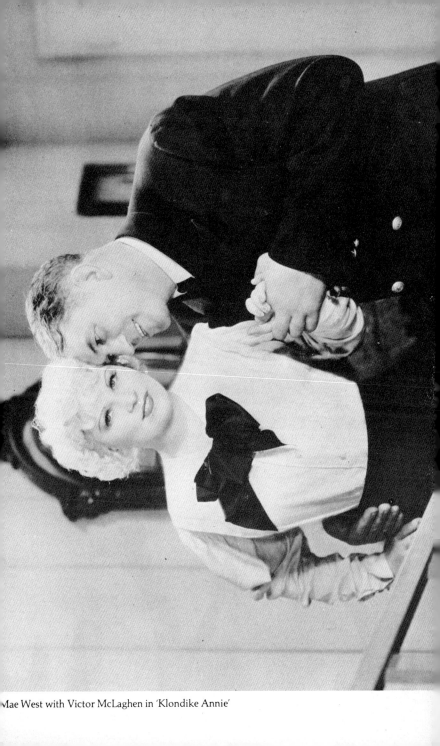

Mae West with Victor McLaghen in 'Klondike Annie'

In 'Klondike Annie', Mae West played Sister Annie in a Mission and caused quite a stir by using dialogue such as 'Give a man a free hand and he'll try to put it all over you'

Mae West with Randolph Scott in a romantic scene from 'Go West, Young Man'

Mae West going for a drive with Charles Butterworth in 'Every Day's a Holiday'

Mae West wore a black wig for her part as Peaches O'Day in 'Every Day's a Holiday'

W C Fields courting Mae West in a scene from 'My Little Chickadee'

Mae West as Flower Belle in 'My Little Chickadee'

Mae West wearing the inevitable diamonds in a scene from 'Tropicana'

A scene from 'Tropicana', a musical extravaganza, starring Mae West with Victor Moore and William Caxton

Mae West, as always, surrounded by men in 'Myra Breckinridge'

The cast of 'Myra Breckinridge' pose between takes: John Huston, Raquel Welch, Mae West and Rex Reed

Mae West's famous line 'Beulah, peel me a grape!' was inspired by her pet monkey Boogie, who meticulously peeled every grape before eating it

Mae West: 'It is better to be looked over than overlooked'

Mae West: 'I've put my cards on the table, but my curves on the couch'. Here she is doing the latter

critic in the Chicago *Herald and Examiner* wrote of the play 'Diamond Lil': 'Never have I seen
actress pawed from hip to buttock as Miss West's avid leading man pawed her in that
droom set . . .'

Mae West with Noel Coward and Cary Grant

Mae West in her costume for the Broadway show 'Catherine was Great'

Mae West arriving at Southampton to star in the play 'Diamond Lil'

Mae West takes a break from the London showing of 'Gay Nineties' to see a selection of her favourite stones at Asprey's in Bond Street

Mae West striking a well-known pose at a press reception held at the Savoy

Mae West at 79, with her secretary Cal Bartlett

Mae West, at 80, seen here with Gerry Lewis and Cal Bartlett

I look pretty buxom and blonde, don't I? Well, believe me, I'm the kind gentlemen prefer.

Gentlemen may prefer blondes – but who says that blondes prefer gentlemen?

I'm no model lady. A model's just an imitation of the real thing.

Everyone has the right to run his own love life – even if you're heading for a crash. What I'm against is blind flying.

Ladies who play with fire must remember that smoke gets in their eyes.

Women with 'pasts' interest men because men hope that history will repeat itself.

Marry in haste; be sued in Reno.

Diamonds are my service stripes.

Opportunity knocks for every man, but you have to give a woman a ring.

Ice is nice at any price.

I never worry about diets. The only carrots that interest me are the number of carats in a diamond.

I'm not hard to please as long as the price is high enough.

A penny saved is a girl lost.

Never judge a man by the spots on his waistcoat. They may conceal a great big heart and a wallet full of gold.

There are no withholding taxes on the wages of sin.

It's got so that if a man opens a door for a lady to go through first, he's the doorman.

The best way to learn to be a lady is to see how other ladies do it.

Let men see what's coming to them, and women will get what's coming to them.

Me wear pants? Me! Why should I when I can wrap myself in slinky silk dresses?

Most men like women when they look like women. You can get a handful of toothpicks in a restaurant – free of charge.

God gave women their curves – effeminate dressmakers took them away by designing garments which could be worn only by women shaped like scarecrows. . . . I think a woman can be slender and yet have curves.

Beauty may only be skin deep, but it's what's underneath that makes the skin beautiful. Keep healthy, and you'll keep good-looking.

If you're trig and trim and straight and wiry, you'll travel in a slam-bang sports roadster; but if you're curved and soft and elegant and grand, you'll ride in a limousine.

On reaching the age of LXX:

I've never considered playing anything but a sexy-looking female, because that's not so old.

The curve is more powerful than the sword.

I didn't discover curves; I only uncovered them.

I'm the regal type – that's not a posture you learn in school, dearie. It's the way you look at the world.

A gal with good lines is better than one with a good line.

When I'm good, I'm very, very good, but when I'm bad, I'm better.

DO YOU KNOW WHAT HAPPENS TO BAD LITTLE GIRLS?

Yeah ... Prosperity!

I like a man who's good, but not too good – for the good die young, and I hate a dead one.

Too much of a good thing can be wonderful.

I'd like to see a woman elected President. Women have been running men for centuries – it would be easy for them to run a country.

Some women pick men to marry – and others pick them to pieces.

When he's young he's interesting – but later he isn't even interested.

A lady may let her hair down as long as the gentleman stands up.

When a girl goes bad – men go right after her.

Good women are no fun. ... The only good woman I can recall in history was Betsy Ross. And all she ever made was a flag.

The harder a girl is to get – the easier she finds it is to get 'em.

I used to be Snow White . . .

. . . but I drifted

A woman in love can't be reasonable – or she probably wouldn't be in love.

Asked if she believed in long or short engagements, Miss West replied:

You can do what you want, but saving love doesn't bring any interest.

Love isn't an emotion or an instinct – it's an art.

Love is the only industry which can't operate on a five-day week.

Women want certain things in marriage – the right to a title and a front seat in the lap of luxury.

Men are easy to get but hard to keep. It takes a better woman to keep the man she has these days than to go out and get a lot of new fellows. . . . Almost any woman can fascinate any man she admires, but can she hold him? It's easy to get married, but hard to stay that way.

In reference to her broken ankle:

There's a rumor goin' round that I broke this thing stumbling over a pile of men.

I'm playing, for the first time in my life, a bedroom act I don't like. The doctor tells me I will have to stay in bed for a few days. And to complicate matters, he has put a No Visitors Allowed sign on my door.

They say I'm running a temperature. But you know me, I always have a little fever.

When she met the founder of the Moral Rearmament Movement, Miss West said:

Have you met W. C. Fields yet? You should. Moral rearmament is just the thing he needs. Give it to him in a bottle and he'll go for it.

When the term 'Mae West', an inflatable life jacket used by airmen during World War II, was put into the dictionary, Miss West remarked:

I've been in *Who's Who*, and I know what's what, but it'll be the first time I ever made the dictionary.

A girl whose curves are knockouts has been known to win on points.

Kiss and make up – but too much makeup has ruined many a kiss.

A girl in the convertible is worth five in the phone book.

Life's just a merry-go-round. Come on up. You might get a brass ring.

An English song called 'If Those Hips Could Only Speak' was written about Miss West. When informed of it, she said:

Whatta they mean 'if they could only speak'? I can make mine talk anytime.

You may admire a girl's curves on first introduction, but the second meeting shows up new angles.

On love and sex:

I take it out in the open and laugh at it.

Sex is like a small business; you gotta protect it, watch over it. A matter of timing.

The best way to hold a man is in your arms.

Brains are an asset to the woman in love who's smart enough to hide 'em.

Look your best – who said love's blind?

Paying a man to dance or keep one company is like hiring somebody to take your bath for you.

An ounce of performance is worth pounds of promises.

Girls, give all your gentlemen friends an even break, even if you have to break them in the attempt.

Cultivate your curves – they may be dangerous but they won't be avoided.

Love thy neighbor – and if he happens to be tall, debonair and devastating, it will be that much easier.

If you put your foot in it, be sure it's your best foot.

It's all right for a perfect stranger to kiss your hand as long as he's perfect.

The best way to behave is to misbehave.

He who hesitates is last.

A man has more character in his face at forty than at twenty – he has suffered longer.

Miss West received a letter from someone wanting to name a gold mine after her. She replied:

Tell him it would be a big mistake – I'm a digger, not a producer.

I'm single because I was born that way.

A dame that knows the ropes isn't likely to get tied up.

Marriage is a great institution. No family should be without it.

I like a man what takes his time.

Don't think a career will replace love – Eden's more fun than a noiseless typewriter.

Don't come crawlin' to a man for love – he likes to get a run for his money.

Don't cry for a man who's left you – the next one may fall for your smile.

Don't sacrifice too much for a man – he never enjoyed anything more than giving up a rib.

Don't marry a man to reform him – that's what reform schools are for.

Don't keep a man guessing too long – he's sure to find the answer somewhere else.

Don't ever make the same mistake twice, unless it pays.

CBS-TV canceled a video-taped Person to Person *interview with Miss West because parts of it 'might be misconstrued'. Interviewer Charles Collingwood commented on all the mirrors in Miss West's plush bedroom. Miss West replied:*

They're for personal observation. I always like to know how I'm doing.

Switching the subject, he suggested they talk about foreign affairs. Miss West said:

I've always had a weakness for foreign affairs.

The following exchange took place on the Red Skelton
Show:

How do you do, Miss West?

How do you do what?

During a Mister Ed *TV appearance Connie Hines said
to Miss West:*

Oh, Miss West, I've heard so much about you.

Miss West replied:

Yeah, honey, but you can't prove a thing.

A fan wrote to Miss West asking if it's true she doesn't smoke or drink. Miss West replied:

It's true, but I don't mind other people smoking or drinking. After all, we can't make love all the time.

QUESTION: Do you like the new styles or the old?

MISS WEST: You can say what you like about long dresses, but they cover a multitude of shins.

Never ask a man where he's been. If he's out on legitimate business, he doesn't need an alibi. And, girls, if he has been out on illegitimate business, it's your own fault.

My secret is positive thinking and no drinking.

Asked by an interviewer the hypothetical question. Would you tell your children 'all', Miss West said:

I would tell my children just so much; then they'd have to find out for themselves. Finding out has its advantages, too.

QUESTION: What kind of man is most satisfactory?

MISS WEST: Personally, I like two types of men – domestic and foreign.

Save a boyfriend for a rainy day – and another, in case it doesn't.

I've been too busy for love, but I love all men.

In my long and colorful career, one thing stands out:
I have been misunderstood.

'I hold records all over the world. That's my ego, breaking records. So don't say they put me in someone else's room.' Mae West was not happy. Her soft voice took on a tense shrillness as she continued. 'I'd like to see someone break records like that and I'll respect them as a star. 'Til someone can do that, I feel I'm in a class by myself. The only other person I know who could write his own movies and star in them was Chaplin. When I had my act with the muscle men in Las Vegas they gave me a diamond bracelet after a two-week run. When they do that you know you're making money for them. All the notables and big-money people came to see me. Someone else had the Coca-Cola crowd.'

The tirade had been triggered by a casual remark that Miss West was getting Barbra Streisand's old dressing room at 20th Century-Fox during the production of 'Myra Breckinridge', Gore Vidal's garden of sexual hybrids. (Miss West is also receiving $350,000, a limousine and top billing over Raquel Welch.) Mae West is seventy-six. She hasn't made a picture in twenty-six years. But in her own mind she is still a movie star, a reigning sex queen. And she does not like to be compared with another woman, even the fellow Brooklynite who did for the nose what Mae West did for the bust. In some ways Miss West is right. She is still there on 'The Late Show', captured forever in her swirls of feathers and diamonds, purring at a practically pubescent Cary Grant, 'Come up and see me sometime'. There is no other Mae West. She is an institution, a living legend, as much a part of American folklore as Paul Bunyan or Tom Sawyer or Babe Ruth.

Visiting such an imposing personage can be a bit unnerving; it's a little like having a chat with Cleopatra. My first interview with Mae West was at her apartment, a small place in a slightly shabby Hollywood building, which she rented when she arrived here in 1932 and has kept ever since. The living room has been described often, but it is still rather startling, all off-white and gilt, fluffy chairs and sofas, ornate pottery lamps with bare-breasted maidens playing lutes, bouquets of dusty flowers, a white piano on which stands a spectacular nude statue of the young Mae West. There are photos of her swathed in furs and feathers, an oil painting of her swathed in nothing but light. This is the stage for her performances, and she keeps you waiting, building up the suspense. When she appears it is in a swirl of pink and green chiffon, bright yellow hair, false eyelashes blackened with mascara. Only slight wrinkles at the corners of her mouth and a puffiness in her throat gave away the secret. She is surprisingly small (about 5 feet 2 inches tall, 124 pounds), despite the famous $43\frac{1}{4}$-inch bust, and soft and feminine. There is nothing she would rather talk about than her own incredible career.

It started back in Bushwick, a family neighborhood of horse-drawn carriages and ragtime music, where Mae West was born on Aug. 17, 1893. From her father, 'Battling Jack' West, a man celebrated for his pugilistic abilities inside and outside the ring, she derived a toughness bordering on belligerency. From her mother, Matilda Delker Doelger, an occasional corset and fashion model, she inherited an anatomy rivaling the structural wonders of the Brooklyn Bridge. She was seven when she persuaded her dancing teacher to enter her in an amateur-night contest sponsored by the local Elks. She was billed as 'Baby Mae – Song and Dance', and she got furious when the spotlight was slow in picking her up. Needless to say, she won the contest. Soon she found a permanent job in Hal Clarendon's stock company at the Gotham Theater in East New York. After a dramatic career studded with such deathless roles as a moonshiner's daughter in the Kentucky hills and a poor white slave in Chinatown, she turned to vaudeville at the age of fourteen.

She worked up a song-and-dance routine with a young jazz singer, Frank Wallace, who, like a good many men, started proposing matrimony. An older woman on the bill advised Mae that her magnetic properties would soon cause her trouble and that marriage would make her 'respectable'. In 1911, at the age of seventeen, before a judge in Milwaukee, she took her marriage vows for the only time in her life. The vows were hardly compelling – she left Wallace within months – but they proved resilient; she did not get a divorce until 1943.

After leaving Wallace she won a featured part in Ned Wayburn's review, 'A La Broadway and Hello, Paris'. On opening night she took seven encores and *The New York Times* reported the next morning that 'a girl named Mae West, hitherto unknown, pleased by her grotesquerie and a snappy way of singing and dancing'. A string of reviews, vaudeville acts and fleeting romances followed swiftly. In 1918 she was playing opposite Ed Wynn in Rudolf Friml's musical 'Sometime', and one night after a performance in Chicago went slumming to a jazz spot on the South Side. She saw black dancers shake with 'a naked, aching, sensual agony' in a dance they called the 'shimmy shawobble'. The next night, when it came time for an encore she introduced the 'shimmy' – eight months before Gilda Gray, who made the dance famous, opened in New York. 'She was a good vaudevillian, but she wasn't good enough to play the Palace,' recalled Don Prince, the theater's former press agent. 'Some genius took her out of second-class vaudeville to first-class Broadway.' That genius was her mother. Here is how Mae remembers the story:

'It was 1926, and the Shuberts were looking for a play for me to do. They couldn't find one and my mother said, "You rewrite all your vaudeville parts, why don't you write your own play?" I had often thought of things, but I was usually too lazy to write them down. This time I didn't want to make a mistake and do something that wasn't right for me, so I sat down and wrote my own play.

'I sent the play over to the Shubert office under the pen name Jane Mast – I didn't want too much Mae West involved. They sent it back – I learned later some girl in the office hadn't even shown it to J. J. Shubert – so my mother said, "Why don't we produce it ourselves and make all the money?" We gave it to a director, who read it and said, "My God, this is what Broadway has been waiting for!" We came back from lunch and I said, "When do we start?" We cast the whole play in a day.

'When we went into rehearsal the director was very excited. He kept saying to me, "You've got something I've never seen in anyone." I finally asked him what it was I had. "You've got a sex quality," he said in this deep voice, "a *low* sex quality." The way he said it, it sounded like the best kind to have. He kept saying the play reeked with sex, sex – he said it so often I began to like the sound of the word. One day I told him I wanted to change the name of the play to "Sex". Up to that time they only used the word in medical textbooks. He said, "Oh, my God, if we only dare," and I said, "I'll dare."'

'Sex', with Mae West in the role of a waterfront prostitute, opened at Daly's Theater on April 27. The *Times* review was not exactly ecstatic: 'A crude, inept play, cheaply produced and poorly acted.' That critic's influence was so great, however, that the play ran for eleven months. In the meantime, its frank sexuality spawned several imitators, and the blue-noses massed their forces. The police raided 'Sex' and two other plays and charged the principals with 'indecent performances'.

Mae West could not have planned things better if she had the most able press agent in New York. She was convicted and spent eight days in the Welfare Island jail. The papers were filled with the cataclysmic news that Miss West's tender skin, so used to silken underwear, was being irritated by the prison's rough cotton garments. She emerged from her incarceration somewhat chafed, perhaps, but a national figure.

Her next play was a study of homosexuality called 'The Drag'. She produced it in such theatrical meccas as Paterson, N. J., but it was so controversial that it never made New York. Miss West has always been particularly popular with homosexuals, perhaps because in her perpetual opulence she looks a bit like a flashy drag queen. 'They're crazy about me because I'm so flamboyant,' she said recently. 'They love to imitate the things I say and the way I act, and they like the way I move my body.'

As her notoriety grew, she wrote and starred in several more plays, including 'Diamond Lil', a musical about a well-kept dance-hall girl on the Bowery of the Gay Nineties. No one accused her of composing great literature, but her performances had a rather stimulating effect on at least one reviewer who gushed: 'So regal is Miss West's manner, so assured is her artistry, so devastating are her charms in the eyes of all red-blooded men, so blonde, so beautiful, so buxom is she that she makes Miss Ethel Barrymore look like the late lamented Mr. Bert Savoy.' The play was later rewritten as a novel and became the basis for 'She Done Him Wrong', the biggest hit among Miss West's ten films. It was no accident. 'Diamond Lil', she said in later years, 'I'm her and she's me and we're each other.'

Broadway was hit hard by the Depression, and in 1932 the talkies lured Mae West to Hollywood. With the typical modesty of the loyal New Yorker, she announced on her arrival: 'I'm not a little girl from a little town making good in a big town. I'm a big girl from a big town making good in a little town.'

The first Mae West picture was 'Night After Night', a gangster epic starring George Raft. Mae insisted that she write her own dialogue, and her very first scene set the pattern for her film career: as she walked into a saloon festooned with glittering gems the hatcheck girl blurted, 'Goodness, what beautiful diamonds.' Mae turned and cracked, 'Goodness had nothing to do with it.' The line became the title of her autobiography. Raft, in his own autobiography, recalled with some displeasure that Miss West 'stole everything but the cameras'.

The movies displayed a new facet of Mae West; she became a comedienne, almost by accident. 'There were a lot of things censors wouldn't let me do in the movies that I had done on the stage,' she recalled. 'They wouldn't even let me sit on a guy's lap – and I'd been on more laps than a napkin. I had to do something different, so I put in some humor. That way I could get away with more things. I never meant "Come up and see me sometime" to be so sexy, but I guess I was thinking about sex all the time. I wasn't conscious of being sexy until the cenors got after me. It was always natural for me, it was never a strain. I guess that's why it goes over so well.'

In her next picture, 'She Done Him Wrong', Mae re-created the role of Diamond Lil, though the name was changed to

Lady Lou for the benefit of the ubiquitous, if not very perceptive, censors, who refused to allow a movie based directly on the play. Production was delayed because Paramount Studios didn't have a leading man. Miss West and some executives were walking on the lot one day and spied a handsome young actor. 'Who's that?' asked Mae. 'His name is Cary Grant,' came the answer. 'He's never made a picture, we just use him for screen tests.' She replied: 'If he can talk, I'll take him.' Grant met the test and won the lead as an undercover agent posing as a Salvation Army captain.

As the sharp-tongued, mushy-hearted girl friend of a saloon-owning political boss, Mae was in top form. 'When women go wrong,' she philosophized, 'men go right after them.' With Grant, the lines whizzed by. 'I'm sorry to be taking your time,' he said. She looked up with a leer: 'What do you think my time is for?' He resisted for the moment, but she sensed a weakness. 'You can be had,' she snapped; then, in a delightful scene, issued her famous invitation to second-story sensuality. Grant seemed shaken by the proposal, and Mae could only laugh. 'Come on up,' she repeated. 'I'll tell your fortune.'

'She Done Him Wrong' was followed quickly by 'I'm No Angel'. In one scene, Mae, upbraided by a wronged wife, ushered the lady out the door, and, burdened by boredom and disdain, turned back to the cameras. 'Beulah,' she called as she sashayed across the screen, 'peel me a grape.'

The two movies made Mae West very famous and very rich. In 1934 she earned $340,000 and the next year $480,833 – it was the second highest salary in the country, exceeded only by that of William Randolph Hearst, who once editorialized, 'Isn't it time Congress did something about Mae West?' Her self-assured swagger, her adenoidal and ungrammatical Brooklynese (one of her best lines was 'diamonds is my ca-re-a,' and she still says 'pernt'), her joyous celebration of sexual delights became known around the world. A grande dame threw a 'Mae West party' at the Eiffel Tower that was the social event of the year. The couturiers quickly picked up her style and ladies of fashion were soon dressing in figure-hugging froufrous of the Gay Nineties. Someone called her 'the figure that launched a thousand hips.' After an appearance on the Edgar Bergen and Charlie McCarthy radio show drew a howl of outrage, N.B.C. paid her the singular compliment of banning her name from the air. Crowds stormed theaters in Vienna protesting her pictures. When she returned to New York for personal appearances, thousands of hysterical fans mobbed her at Penn Station. She entered the dictionary when British airmen used her name for an inflatable life jacket that somewhat resembled her awesome chest. Princeton scientists designed a new magnet in the shape of her torso. Everyone from college boys to women newspaper reporters voted her the most popular actress. A New York newspaper ran a six-part series proclaiming 'This Mae Westian Age'.

Why was it a Mae Westian Age? 'There had been sex sirens before, like Theda Bara, but she was so sexy she was sinister,' said Stanley Musgrove, a producer and close friend of Mae West. 'They all portrayed sex as a heavy, evil thing. Mae was breezy and humorous. It was the first instance of blatant camp. I don't think she knew what she was doing, it was just there.' Miss West described her impact this way in her autobiography: 'Women became more sex-conscious, and this, for some men, was a big break; for others, a bother. Sex was out in the open and amusing.' The censors and other guardians of public morals did not share in the gaiety, but from Mae West's viewpoint, she had always been something of a put-on. 'I make fun of vulgarity,' she said. 'I kid sex.'

In her career, as in her comedy, Mae West showed good timing. 'You feel good when you're around her, and that imparts itself on the screen,' said Robert Fryer, the producer of 'Myra Breckinridge'. 'That's why she was such a success in the Depression. She really made people forget their troubles.' Douglas Gilbert, writing in the *New York World-Telegram* in 1933, thought Mae West symbolized a revolt against the 'modern' woman of emancipated ideas and emaciated shape who had dominated the twenties:

'No argument can dislodge her present position. She has given the gate to those proud beauties who once ruled our screen. The great Garbo today is a trifle passé. "Legs" Dietrich, as she is dubbed in the studios, shakes her slender limbs to apathetic houses. ... Against Mae's ample bosom figuratively rest the modish aspirations of our girls. Her well-rounded arms encircle a nation's desire for escape from a synthetic life to one of substance and color.'

In all of her pictures Mae West played essentially the same

character – herself. But sometimes she was like the mirrors in a barbershop: an almost infinite number of images, each reflecting the other, Mae West playing Mae West playing Mae West. The character usually had a big build-up, fancy clothes (often diamonds) and considerable power. She was always the center of attention. She was never a mother or an aunt, seldom a wife, usually an illicit girl friend. 'My fans,' said Miss West, 'expect certain things of me.' She wrote virtually all of her own dialogue, and to her it did not matter that the characters were so similar. 'It is not what you do,' she said many times, in many contexts, 'but how you do it.'

'Too much of a good thing,' she once remarked, 'can be wonderful.' But gradually the critics and the public began to disagree. As the thirties waned, so did Mae West. Even 'My Little Chickadee', her famous encounter with W. C. Fields (whom she detested for his drunkenness), was panned when it appeared in 1939. One critic saw her final picture, 'The Heat's On', in 1943 and wrote 'The heat is definitely off.' After that Mae turned back to the stage. She toured the country in several mediocre plays of her own composition and revived 'Diamond Lil' in London and New York; while the crowds were enthusiastic, they seemed interested in her mainly as a historical curiosity. 'Like Chinatown and Grant's Tomb,' one critic wrote, 'Mae West should be seen at least once.'

In the mid-fifties she put together a night-club act that spoofed the girlie shows: eight muscle men in loincloths and Mae, resplendent in her 'Diamond Lil' finery, adored by them all. Recently there have been a few television guest shots and several rock 'n' roll record albums, but little else. She received a few movie offers but turned them down. Occasionally the papers announced that she would appear in a new TV series or play, but the projects never seemed to come off.

While her career declined, however, her old films enjoyed a revival among youngsters who were not even born when she made her last picture. When 'She Done Him Wrong' and 'I'm No Angel' shared a double bill recently in Hollyood, they outgrossed any new picture issued by Universal Studios, which owns her old prints. Part of the reason is the campiness, the outrageous exaggeration – Mae West as a pop poster. Moreover, like Fields and Bogart, she had a flip insolence and self-assurance that appeals to an iconoclastic generation. She is, after all, the woman who said such things as 'Good women

90

are no fun. ... The only good woman I can recall in history was Betsy Ross, and all she ever made was a flag.' Arthur Knight, the film critic and historian, feels there is also an element of escapism in her resurgence: 'She's part of a whole enthusiasm for the thirties, along with Fields and the Marx Brothers and Bogart. The kids are looking back at a time that seemed freer and easier – no wars or race problems, just nice gangsters. And I think they feel a little guilty about being part of an affluent society. Look at all the jeans and raggedy shirts they wear – it's kind of a do-it-yourself Depression.'

Mae West says she is coming back to the movies 'because my fans have been pleading and demanding for me to come back.' Maybe that's true, but there is an element of sadness in it all. Many of her fans seem to be demanding what she was, not what she is. Our idea of glamour has changed radically – indeed, even the word is outmoded. Raquel Welch poses for publicity photos in torn shirts, the grubbier the better; Mae was never photographed in anything but a full-length gown. Movie stars are less important and more realistic today; Mae West was always outsized, larger than life. She is fine as a period piece, rather out of place as a contemporary.

But Mae West feels no pity for herself. She owns considerable real estate (a Hollywood apartment, a beach house in Santa Monica and a ranch in the San Fernando Valley) and a large collection of diamonds (when she wears some of her better stuff the insurance company sends along a guard). She lives alone, but has the constant attention of Paul Novak, a former muscle man in her nightclub act, who serves as chauffeur, butler and general handyman. Her private life remains, as always, very private. She has spun a cocoon for herself and nestled inside, largely unaware of and unconcerned about the world.

Her day is very orderly. She gets up late, goes over fan mail, tends to business and personal calls, often rides to her beach house or to the ranch, where her sister, Beverly, now lives. (Most of her fan letters – she gets 200 a week – come from younger people who see her movies on television; a sizable number contain the flowery rhetoric of a rather obvious homosexual. However, one recent letter from a professor at Brown University said he used a collection of her 'wit and wisdom' in his English course.) Occasionally, Miss West does some writing, and she has several screen plays finished. She left school at 13 and seldom reads. The architect who designed her beach house once returned for a visit and noticed that she had ripped out a set of bookcases. 'They look pretty silly without books,' she explained.

In the evening she occasionally goes to a movie or has dinner with such friends as George Cukor, the director, or Robert Wise, who is producing a TV special for her. (Though many of her pictures were set in saloons, Miss West has always disliked liquor. As a young girl she sampled some strong spirits and had a bad fight with her mother, whom she adored; the morning after she swore off booze.) Several years ago, Cukor arranged a dinner party at which he introduced Garbo and West to each other. Mae, who is often nervous around other women, was apprehensive as the time approached. 'What will Garbo want to talk about?' she asked Cukor. Then she brightened: 'If she's anything like me, she'll talk about herself.'

According to reports, Garbo arrived late and was somewhat startled when Mae kissed her on the cheek. 'I wanted her to feel at ease,' Mae explained. Said a friend: 'Garbo of course, was more interested in Mae than Mae was in Garbo, so Mae spent most of the evening talking about her career. Garbo wanted to know especially about her muscle men.'

Mae West's overriding interest is the care and feeding of Mae West. 'My secret is positive thinking and no drinking,' she once said, but it involves more than that. She exercises continually – with small bar bells, a walking machine, a stationary bicycle. She has been called 'a Mount Rushmore of the cosmetician's art', and the pampering of her face, hair, nails and teeth take up a good part of her day. She eats lean meat and salads; she does not smoke and dislikes others to smoke around her. When she is at the beach or the ranch, she takes long walks. 'I sometimes see her in the evening, after the crowds have gone,' said a neighbor in Santa Monica. 'She walks along the beach on the arm of a man and is usually wearing his coat to keep warm. When I see her on the street she is all porcelain and perfect, but on the beach she shuffles a little, like an old woman.'

Miss West is used to being worshipped, and when I paid my first visit she was a little nervous at the presence of a stranger who was not yet a card-carrying idolator. 'I am the greatest screen personality since Valentino,' she said, striving to establish her eminence. 'I didn't say that, though; the studio did.' What had she been doing recently? 'I've lived the same way ever since I can remember. I concentrate on myself most of the time. Everything I do pertains to myself. Everything I wrote, like "Catherine Was Great", was for me.' Did she star in that? She laughed. 'I star in everything.'

The mention of the Catherine play, which she opened in 1944, started her reminiscing about the years after World War II. 'When I wrote that, Lee Shubert called up and said, "I'm sending out a guy to produce it. He's not too smart, but he'll run his legs off for you." It was Mike Todd. That ran for a few years and then I wrote a new play, "Come On Up". They wanted me to bring it to New York but I didn't want to work that hard and I closed it down. I also wrote a screen version of "The Drag". They're ready for that now. I was always ahead of my time. I wrote "The Constant Simmer" in the late twenties – the story of a black man and a white woman. I'm always thinking of what I'm going to do next. At 17 I was the youngest headliner in vaudeville and I wrote all my own plays and movies and my autobiography. I've always been two people. Most stars are just told what to think, but I told the director what to think.'

We were interrupted by costume people from the studio. Miss West's role in 'Myra' is Letitia Van Allen, an actor's agent who holds many of her auditions in a huge bed in her office. The clothes were all black and white – tunics and pajamas and flowing coats. We were called into the bedroom for a showing. There was the famous bed with the mirror on the ceiling ('I always like to see how I'm doing,' she once explained) and a set of white bar bells in the corner. 'What, no pockets?' she said, striking a jaunty pose in a pants suit. A studio aide hustled to make a note. Another change, and Mae was in a kidding mood. Her voice dropped to that nasal whine, her hand went to her hip and she drawled the first line of her part, 'Awright, boys, get your résumés ready.' But the clothes weren't right. 'I look like a house,' she kept muttering. Someone objected. 'You aren't wearing a corset now, are you?' She snapped back, 'Of course I'm wearing a girdle.'

After the fitting, she had appointments with a manicurist and a hairdresser. We arranged to meet a week later at Perino's, her favorite restaurant, a richly appointed and richly priced place that, in typical Los Angeles fashion, offers an odd mixture of French, Italian and American dishes.

Mae arrived in a floor-length white gown with semi-precious stones at the neck and wrists. Two huge diamonds glittered on a ring and smaller stones shone forth from a bracelet. As she entered slowly on Paul Novak's arm, she looked, in her own word, 'regal'.

We talked about her childhood in Brooklyn ('Sunday school always gave me a headache') and her parents, an indulgent mother and an irascible father. 'I had a mother who thought I was the greatest thing on earth,' she recalled. 'By the time I was 12 I had a lot of boyfriends and she would always let them come in the house. One of my boyfriends was Joe Schenk, of the vaudeville team of Schenk and Van – his mother was a nurse in our house for a while. I've always had multiple men in my life; that's been the pattern ever since I was a child. That's how I can write parts in pictures for five or six men; I had that in real life. Once my cousin told my father that I was staying out late with the boys and he was furious. He came home and I picked up an iron rod he kept near his bed. I thought he was going to hit me and I was going to hit him first, but he never touched me.'

During most of her career, Miss West managed to keep her private life so secluded that newspaper stories of the day said she had never been 'romantically linked' with anyone. In her autobiography she frankly recounted a long series of often brief affairs. 'If Kinsey is right,' she wrote, 'I have only done what comes naturally, what the average American does secretly, drenching himself in guilt fixations and phobias because of his sense of sinning. I have never felt myself a sinner or committed what I would call a sin.'

Did she regret never having settled down and had children? 'I never wanted children. I thought it would change me – mentally, physically and psychologically. I was always too absorbed in myself and I didn't have time for anybody else. I was talked into marriage once and maybe it was a good thing – I might have gotten married 10 times if I had been free all those years. But you know, a woman becomes a different person

94

when she gets married. She lives for her husband and her family. I wanted to live for myself.' ('She says she never wanted to be a mother,' observes her friend Stanley Musgrove, 'but you should see her with her pet monkeys. She calls them "baby" and cuddles them like kids. It's a tip-off on how she really feels.' She is so devoted to her monkeys that when one was sent to a kennel she visited regularly and sent fruit. She also financed an eye operation for one of the monkey's kennel playmates.)

The subject drifted to current movies. 'They haven't got the glamour any more,' she said between forkfuls of crab legs in mustard sauce. 'Even in clothes and cars they don't have glamour. Take a Ford, it looks the same as a Cadillac, there's no distinction left. It's even true of diamonds. There are so many good phony ones on the market anyone can wear them and be happy ...

'I don't think nudity is sexy. Now they're doing it because they have to change. There were so many great pictures in the thirties and forties and fifties, so many great stars and directors. They don't have that today – to be a star you have to be a little better than anyone else. All the great plots have been done, so they have to slap something together and throw in a naked body. I saw a picture recently, I think it was called "Childish Things". They have a nude woman riding a carousel and a rape scene. It didn't do anything for me. Take the "Sound of Music". That was great. It didn't have all the noise and confusion and crazy lights they have now, but it made a lot of money; people will come to see that sort of thing.'

I asked her how she had liked the book 'Myra Breckinridge', whose main character changes sex several times in the course of the story. 'It didn't grab me,' she replied; but later she confessed: 'I didn't even read the damn script all the way through, it was too much work. I've just been working on my part. I lie down every day and scribble lines on little pieces of paper, and when I have enough of them I put them together for a scene. I can tell you that I have affairs with all the leading men and I finish up owning everything. My fans would be disappointed otherwise.' Among the other stars of the movie are Miss Welch, who plays Myra, a rapacious young woman on the make in Hollywood, and Rex Reed, the celebrated interviewer ('Do You Sleep in the Nude'), who makes his screen debut as Myron – Myra before her sex-change operation.

Miss West is writing all of her own dialogue for 'Myra', and Fryer, the producer, is still a little surprised that he approved the arrangement. 'I would never do it for anyone else,' he explained, 'but no one can write Mae West's dialogue better than Mae West.'

We talked about her health secrets. 'You have to be healthy on the inside or else it shows on the outside,' she said as raspberries and cream showed up for dessert. 'You have to eat good and not go to extremes. You know, I was born with a double thyroid – they stimulate your sex glands and everything. I guess that's why I have so much energy. And I don't do anything that's bad for me. I don't like to be made nervous or angry. Any time you get upset it tears down your nervous system. That's why I have only "yes" men around me. Who needs "no" men?'

Mae urged Paul Novak to order a piece of chocolate cake, and he reluctantly agreed. When she finished her berries, she coquettishly stole a bite from him. The whole idea of a 76-year-old woman flirting left me rather stunned, but I asked one last question, what she wanted to be remembered for. She didn't hesitate. 'Everything.'